THE NEW EARTH
YOU'RE GONNA LOVE IT!

Written by Kathi DeCanio
Illustrated by Phillip Ortiz

LET THE CHILDREN PRESS

The New Earth
copyright© 2019 Kathi DeCanio
All rights reserved

ISBN: 978-0-9892016-3-6

letthechildrenpress@gmail.com
letthechildrenpress.wordpress.com

I dedicate this book to my daughter, Sophia, and my son, Matthew, who have anchored their daily lives in the "all that is to come" in eternity on the New Earth, who make their choices based not on what will give them advancement in this life, but on what is valuable in the eyes of the Lord and has eternal value and reward.

When Jesus Returns

Did you ever wonder what will happen
to the world when Jesus comes back
again? Will He take us all back to heaven
to live there with Him forever? Will we live
in heaven? What will happen to the earth?
The Apostle John, near the end of the book
of Revelation, tells us,

*"Then I saw a new heaven and a new earth...
I saw the holy city—the new Jerusalem—
coming down out of heaven from God...
I heard a loud voice from the throne saying:
'Look! The home of God is among human
beings. He will live among them, and they
will be His people, and God Himself will
be with them.'"*
(Revelation 21:1-3)

Isn't that amazing? After Jesus removes all the evil from the world and the only people on earth are people who love Him, worship Him, and obey Him, God the Father comes to us! Satan and his demons will be thrown into the lake of fire forever. The Lord God Almighty will make His home forever with us.

What will earth be like when God comes to live here with us? Let's look at what God has shown us in the Bible about this.

Jerusalem, The Capital of the World

When David became king over all Israel, he made Jerusalem his new capital city. Then the Lord made David a very unique promise. He said that someone from David's family—his great-great-great-many-times-great-grandson would one day sit on the throne in Jerusalem and rule over all the nations forever.

David did not know who this man would be. He didn't know how God would do this. But David believed God. He didn't know that one day Jesus would be born to his many-times great-granddaughter Mary or that Jesus would be the promised Messiah, the Savior of the world. He didn't know that Jesus would be the Son of God and would rule the world forever. But he believed God it would happen.

Now, not only had God chosen David and his family to be the family for His Son, but God had also chosen the city of Jerusalem to be the place where He Himself would live forever.

Certainly the Lord chose Zion, Jerusalem. He decided to make it his home. He said, "This will be my resting place forever. I will live here, for I have chosen it." (Ps. 132: 13-14, NET)

Eight hundred years before Jesus came, Isaiah told us about God's plans for Jerusalem. He wrote about the time when Jesus, the Messiah, would rule from Jerusalem, the mountain of the Lord.

Many peoples shall say, "Come on! Let's go up to the mountain of the Lord, to the house of the God of Jacob. The Lord will teach us His ways, and we will walk in His paths, for out of Zion the laws of God shall go forth and the word of the Lord will be spoken from Jerusalem." (Isaiah 2:3)

Isaiah told us more about life in Jerusalem when Jesus rules there. He said,

Then wolves will live in peace with lambs, and leopards will lie down to rest with goats. Calves, lions and young bulls will eat together, and a little child will lead them. Cows and bears will eat together in peace. Their young will lie down together. Lions will eat hay as oxen do...They will not hurt or destroy each other on all my holy mountain. The earth will be full of the knowledge of the Lord, as the sea is full of water. (Isa. 11:6-9, ICB)

Can you imagine that? The wolf living peacefully with the little lambs? Lions eating hay with cows and their babies? You will be able to pet the lions, and the tigers, and the bears! Oh my! Won't that be amazing?

We will even go camping and sleep under the stars!

I will make a covenant of peace with them and will rid the land of wild beasts, so that they can live securely in the wilderness and even sleep in the woods. I will turn them and the regions around My hill, Jerusalem, into a blessing.

(Ezekiel 34:25-26, NET)

The New Jerusalem, The Home of the Father

What do you think a city would look like if God built it? That's what Abraham was looking for, you know.

He left his own country, not knowing where he was to go. It was by faith that he lived in the country God promised to give him... He lived in tents with Isaac and Jacob, who had received that same promise from God. Abraham was waiting for the city that has real foundations— the city planned and built by God.

(Hebrews 11:8-10, ICB)

How would God build a city? What would He build it out of? Guess what? The Apostle John saw the New Jerusalem. It is the city that Abraham was waiting for! John told us what it looks like.

The city's wall is made of jasper
and the city is pure gold,
like transparent glass.

The foundations of the city's wall are
decorated with every kind of precious
stone. (Revelation 21:18-19, NET)

The first foundation is jasper,
the second sapphire,
the third agate,
the fourth emerald,
the fifth onyx
the sixth carnelian
the seventh chrysolite
the eighth beryl
the ninth topaz
the tenth chrysoprase
the eleventh jacinth
and the twelfth amethyst
(Revelation 21:19-20, NET)

Can you imagine that? A city made of gold? Decorated with beautiful gemstones? Wait until you see the city gates!

This city has twelve great, big gates, three on each side. Each gate is made from a gigantic pearl! Stationed at every gate is a great angel.

Inside the city there is a great river. It is not just any river. No, this is the River of Life that flows from the throne of God. You will see trees on each side of this magnificent river. These aren't just any tree, either. No, this is the tree of life, just like in the Garden of Eden. Now, apple trees, pear trees, and all fruit trees bear their fruit once a year. Not the tree of life! It bears fruit every month! Can you imagine that? Even the leaves of the tree of life are special. The angel told John that the leaves would heal the nations. Such a special tree!

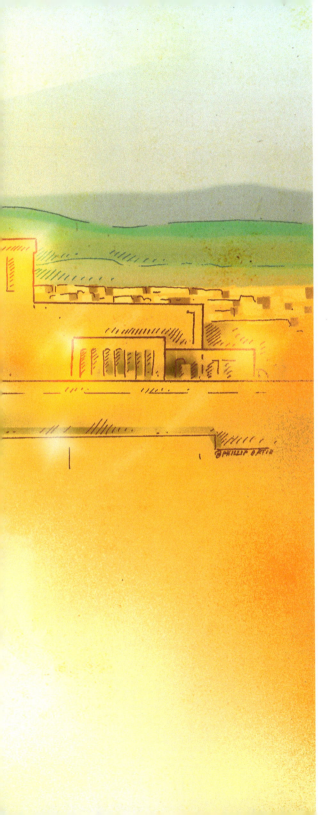

There is something else very special about the New Jerusalem. Inside the city, there is no need for lights. You see, the Lord will live there, His throne will be there, and the brightness of His person will light up the entire city. He shines brighter than the sun!

What do you think will be happening outside the New Jerusalem, in the rest of Israel and in the rest of the earth? You remember that River of Life? Well, it flows out of the city, then splits in two. Half of it flows to the Mediterranean Ocean. Half of it flows to the Jordan River and all the way to the Dead Sea. But when the water of the River of Life enters the Dead Sea, it won't be dead any longer! That sea will be full of fish! All along the river banks, all the plants and trees will grow full and strong, just like in the Garden of Eden.

In fact, all of the earth will become beautiful like the Garden of Eden. Won't that be lovely?

You see, the angel also told John that there would be no curse. Remember when Adam and Eve disobeyed God in the Garden of Eden and ate fruit from the Tree of the Knowlege of Good and Evil? One of the consequences of their disobedience is that God put a curse on the ground so that man had to work very hard for food.

In the new earth, the curse has been removed because Jesus has removed evil from the earth. Fruit and vegetables will grow easily. Meaning, you will have time to explore the new earth.

We will help Jesus take care of the animals and the plants all over the earth! You know what's the best thing?

No one will die anymore, not even the animals!
You will make friends with cats and dogs, monkeys
and squirrels, and you will be friends forever!

We will sing and dance as we worship Jesus forever. You will play instruments like drums, guitar, piano, and many others.

We will play games, too, like tag, soccer, and baseball. Imagine, we will learn games from people who lived 1000 years ago and loved Jesus like we do. Won't that be fun?

Best of all, our hearts will be full of the love of Jesus. We will feel how much He loves us. We will be full of love for Him all the time. And, we will love each other. No fighting. Just loving and helping each other. *Forever.*

LET THE CHILDREN PRESS

CPSIA information can be obtained
at www.ICGtesting.com
Printed in the USA
BVHW021655301221
625231BV00002B/12